# THE WORLD CUP TRIVIA QUIZ BOOK

**350 Questions on the History of the World Cup**

Compiled by Carl Franks

Unauthorised and Unofficial

First published in 2014 by Apex Publishing Ltd
12A St. John's Road, Clacton on Sea
Essex, CO15 4BP, United Kingdom
www.apexpublishing.co.uk

Please email any queries to Chris Cowlin: mail@apexpublishing.co.uk

Print layout by
Andrews UK Limited
www.andrewsuk.com

Copyright © 2014 Carl Franks

The authors have asserted their moral rights

All rights reserved. This book is sold subject to the condition, that no part of this book is to be reproduced, in any shape or form. Or by way of trade, stored in a retrieval system or transmitted in any form or by any means, electronic, mechanical, photocopying, recording, be lent, re-sold, hired out or otherwise circulated in any form of binding or cover other than that in which it is published and without a similar condition, including this condition being imposed on the subsequent purchaser, without prior permission of the copyright holder.

# Contents

| | |
|---|---|
| **Questions** | 1 |
| Uruguay - 1930 | 2 |
| Italy - 1934 | 3 |
| France - 1938 | 4 |
| Brazil - 1950 | 5 |
| Switzerland - 1954 | 6 |
| Sweden - 1958 | 7 |
| Chile - 1962 | 9 |
| England - 1966 | 11 |
| Mexico - 1970 | 13 |
| West Germany - 1974 | 15 |
| Argentina - 1978 | 17 |
| Spain - 1982 | 19 |
| Mexico - 1986 | 21 |
| Italy - 1990 | 23 |
| USA - 1994 | 25 |
| France - 1998 | 27 |
| Japan and South Korea - 2002 | 29 |
| Germany - 2006 | 31 |
| South Africa - 2010 | 33 |
| Goal Scorers | 35 |
| World Cup Stadiums and Venues | 37 |
| World Cup Firsts | 39 |
| World Cup Milestones | 41 |
| World Cup Legends | 43 |
| World Cup Trivia | 45 |

| | |
|---|---|
| **Answers** | 47 |
| Uruguay - 1930 | 48 |
| Italy - 1934 | 49 |
| France - 1938 | 50 |
| Brazil - 1950 | 51 |
| Switzerland - 1954 | 52 |
| Sweden - 1958 | 53 |
| Chile - 1962 | 54 |
| England - 1966 | 55 |
| Mexico - 1970 | 56 |
| West Germany - 1974 | 57 |
| Argentina - 1978 | 58 |
| Spain - 1982 | 59 |
| Mexico - 1986 | 60 |
| Italy - 1990 | 61 |
| USA - 1994 | 62 |
| France - 1998 | 63 |
| Japan and South Korea - 2002 | 64 |
| Germany - 2006 | 65 |
| South Africa - 2010 | 66 |
| Goal Scorers | 67 |
| World Cup Stadiums and Venues | 68 |
| World Cup Firsts | 69 |
| World Cup Milestones | 70 |
| World Cup Legends | 71 |
| World Cup Trivia | 72 |

# THE WORLD CUP
# TRIVIA QUIZ BOOK

# Questions

# Uruguay - 1930

1. Who did Uruguay beat 4-2 in the final of the 1930 World Cup to become the first ever World Champions?

2. How many teams competed in the 1930 World Cup?

3. Which city hosted all games during the 1930 World Cup?

4. What was the nationality of the Golden Boot winner, Guillermo Stabile?

5. How many games were played during the 1930 World Cup?

6. Which country scored the most goals during the 1930 World Cup?

7. How many players did Uruguay have in the All Star team of 1930?

8. Who presented the trophy to the winning captain in 1930?

9. Which team finished top of group 4 in 1930? *A: Paraguay B: Belgium C: USA D: Brazil*

10. Who was the only European team to make it to the semi finals in 1930?

# Italy - 1934

11. Who did Italy beat 2-1 in the final of the 1934 World Cup?

12. How many teams competed in the 1934 World Cup?

13. Which city hosted the 1934 World Cup Final?

14. Which team beat Austria 3-2 to clinch 3rd place in the first ever 3rd / 5th Place Play Off?

15. What was the nationality of the 1934 leading goal scorer, Oldrich Nejedly?

16. Who beat Spain in 1-0 in the first ever replay in a World Cup match?

17. How many own-goals were scored during the 1934 World Cup?

18. Which country became the first African team to participate at a World Cup in 1934?

19. How many South American teams qualified for the quarter finals in the 1934 World Cup?

20. Who did Italy beat 7-1 in the first round of the 1934 World Cup? *A: Bolivia B: USA C: Mexico D: Spain*

# France - 1938

21. Who did Italy beat 4-2 in the final of the 1938 World Cup?

22. How many teams competed in the 1938 World Cup?

23. Who beat Sweden 4-2 to finish 3rd at the 1938 World Cup?

24. In total, how many cities hosted matches during the 1938 World Cup?

25. What was the nationality of the 1938 leading goal scorer, Leonidas?

26. Which country scored the most goals during the 1938 World Cup?

27. Which country became the first Asian team to participate at a World Cup in 1938?

28. Which Caribbean team made its first and only appearance at the 1938 World Cup?

29. Which country was prevented from participating at the 1938 World Cup due to War?

30. Who did Brazil beat 6-5 in the first round of the 1938 World Cup? *A: Austria B: Poland C: Switzerland D: Belgium*

# Brazil - 1950

31. Which stadium hosted the opening game of the 1950 World Cup?

32. How many teams competed in the 1950 World Cup?

33. Who did Uruguay beat 2-1 in the final match of the 1950 World Cup?

34. Who officially finished third in the 1950 World Cup?

35. In total, how many cities hosted matches during the 1950 World Cup?

36. What was the nationality of the 1950 World Cup leading goal scorer?

37. Germany and which other country were banned from competing in the 1950 World Cup?

38. Which team finished top of group 1 in 1950? *A: Yugoslavia B: Switzerland C: Mexico D: Brazil*

39. Which country qualified for its first and so far only World Cup in 1950 but withdrew before the tournament started, citing 'financial reasons'?

40. Which future winner of the World Cup made their debut in the competition in 1950?

# Switzerland - 1954

41. Who did West Germany beat 3-2 in the final of the 1954 World Cup after being beaten 8-3 by them earlier in the tournament?

42. Who beat Uruguay 3-1 to finish 3rd in the 3rd / 4th Place Play Off?

43. Which city hosted the 1954 World Cup Final?

44. What was the nationality of the Golden Boot winner, Sandor Kocsis?

45. Which country became the first to be eliminated by a toss of a coin following a 2-2 draw with Turkey?

46. Which country scored the most goals during the 1958 World Cup?

47. What was the name of the 1954 Golden Ball winner, also known as 'The Galloping Major?

48. Which Asian country made its World Cup debut in 1954?

49. Who did Brazil beat 5-0 in the first round in 1954?

50. Which South American country participated on European soil for the first time at the 1954 World Cup?

# Sweden - 1958

51. Who did Brazil beat 5-2 in the final of the 1958 World Cup?

52. Who scored the fourth Brazilian goal in the 1958 World Cup Final?

53. What nationality was the referee in the 1958 World Cup Final?

54. Who beat West Germany 6-3 to finish 3rd in the 3rd / 4th Place Play Off?

55. How many stadiums were used for the 1958 World Cup?

56. How many matches did Just Fontaine score in on his way to winning the Golden Boot in 1958?

57. What was the name of the England captain during the 1958 World Cup?

58. Who beat Argentina 6-1 in the first round of the 1958 World Cup?

59. How many hat-tricks were scored during the 1958 World Cup?

60. Which European team failed to qualify for the World Cup for the first and only time in 1958?

61. The first 0-0 draw in a World Cup took place in 1958 between England and which other country?

62. Which team finished top of group 3 in 1958? *A: Argentina B: Northern Ireland C: Czechoslovakia D: West Germany*

63. Which team from the British Isles competed in their first and so far only World Cup in 1958?

64. How old was Pele when he scored his first ever World Cup goal in 1958?

65. Which club was Ferenc Puskas playing for at the time of the 1958 World Cup?

# Chile - 1962

66. Who did Brazil beat 3-1 in the final of the 1962 World Cup?

67. Who scored the first Brazilian goal in the 1962 World Cup Final?

68. Who did Chile beat 1-0 in the 3rd / 4th Place Play Off?

69. Who won the Golden Ball award for Player of the Tournament in 1962?

70. Which South American team made their World Cup debut in 1962?

71. Who did Hungary beat 6-1 in the first round of the 1962 World Cup?

72. How many venues were used in the 1962 World Cup?

73. Which country scored the most goals at the 1962 World Cup?

74. How many players were sent off in the match between Italy and Chile, known as 'The Battle of Santiago'?

75. Who were Brazil's opponents when Pele got injured in the first round, forcing him to miss the rest of the tournament?

76. How many European teams reached the quarter finals of the 1962 World Cup?

77. Which team finished top of group 2 in 1962? *A: Italy B: Switzerland C: Chile D: West Germany*

78. Which team did Bobby Charlton score his first ever World Cup goal against in 1962?

79. How many goals did Garrincha score during the 1962 World Cup?

80. How many goals did Lev Yashin concede during the 1962 World Cup?

# England - 1966

81. Who did England beat 4-2 in the final of the 1966 World Cup?

82. Who scored the third English goal in the 1966 World Cup Final?

83. What was the name of the World Cup winning captain in 1966?

84. Who beat the Soviet Union 2-1 to finish 3rd in the 1966 World Cup?

85. Other than Wembley, which stadium hosted a semi final in the 1966 World Cup Finals?

86. Brazil only won one game in the 1966 World Cup, who did they beat in the first round?

87. Who won the Golden Boot in 1966?

88. How many English players made it into the All Star team of the 1966 World Cup?

89. Which Asian team made its debut in 1966?

90. The 1966 World Cup had the lowest number of goals scored at an average of 2.78 per match in any World Cup to this point, how many were scored in total?

91. Who won the Golden Ball at the 1966 World Cup?

92. What nationality was the referee in the 1966 World Cup?

93. How many African nations participated in the 1966 World Cup?

94. Which team from Europe made its first appearance at a World Cup in 1966?

95. How many goals did Franz Beckenbauer score in the 1966 World Cup?

# Mexico - 1970

96. Who did Brazil beat 4-1 in the final of the 1970 World Cup?

97. Who scored the third Brazilian goal in the 1970 World Cup Final?

98. What was the name of the World Cup winning captain in 1970, who also became the first winning captain to score in a final?

99. Who did Germany beat 1-0 in the 3rd / 4th Place Play Off?

100. Which stadium hosted the 1970 World Cup Final?

101. Who won the Golden Boot in 1970?

102. Who became the first winners of the FIFA Fair Play Award in 1970?

103. Yellow and Red cards were introduced for the first time in the 1970 tournament, how many red cards were issued?

104. How many hat-tricks were scored during the 1970 World Cup?

105. Who won the Golden Ball for Player of the Tournament at the 1970 World Cup?

106. How many Brazilian players made the All Star Team in 1970?

107. How many matches went into extra time in 1970?

108. Which country beat El Salvador 4-0 in the first round, recording only its second ever victory in their 7$^{th}$ World Cup appearance?

109. Which African team made its first appearance at the World Cup in 1970?

110. How many goals did Pele score in the 1970 World Cup?

# West Germany - 1974

111. Who did West Germany beat 2-1 in the final of the 1974 World Cup?

112. What was the name of the captain who lifted the FIFA World Cup trophy for the first time in 1974?

113. What was the nationality of the referee who controversially awarded a penalty in the 1974 World Cup Final after 1 minute?

114. Who beat Brazil 1-0 to finish third in the 3rd / 4th Place Play Off?

115. Which city hosted the 1974 World Cup Final?

116. Who won the Golden Boot in 1974?

117. Who was the Dutch coach during 1974 who was credited with the invention of 'Total Football' and named 'FIFA Coach of the Century' in 1999?

118. Australia made their World Cup debut in 1974, what's the nickname of their football team?

119. Which European nation, that is no longer in existence, made its one and only appearance at a World Cup in 1974, beating eventual champions West Germany 1-0 in the first round?

120. Who was the captain of Scotland during the 1974 World Cup?

121. Who won the Golden Ball at the 1974 World Cup?

122. How many stadiums were used during the 1974 World Cup?

123. Who did Argentina beat 4-1 in their first round Group 4 clash in 1974?

124. Which African team made their first appearance at a World Cup in 1974 and would appear again in 2010 as Democratic Republic of Congo?

125. Which West German goalkeeper was selected for the FIFA All Star Team at the 1974 World Cup?

# Argentina - 1978

126. Who did Argentina beat 3-1 in the final of the 1978 World Cup?

127. Who scored the first Argentina goal in the 1978 World Cup Final?

128. What was the name of the World Cup winning captain in 1978?

129. Who did Brazil beat 2-1 in the 3rd / 4th Place Play Off?

130. Which stadium hosted the 1978 World Cup Final?

131. Who won the Golden Boot and Golden Ball double in 1978?

132. Who did West Germany beat 6-0 in their first round Group 2 match in 1978?

133. What was the name of the West German captain during the 1978 World Cup?

134. How many games went to Extra Time at the 1978 World Cup?

135. Which country won the FIFA Fair Play award in 1978?

136. Which team finished top of group 3 in 1978? *A: Brazil B: Spain C: Sweden D: Austria*

137. Who did Argentina controversially beat 6-0 in the second round to ensure their passage through to the 1978 World Cup Final?

138. Which European club did World Cup winning manager Cesar Luis Menotti go on to manage after leaving Argentina in 1982?

139. Which country did Michel Platini score his first ever World Cup goal against during the first round in 1978?

140. Which African team made their debut at the 1978 World Cup?

# Spain - 1982

141. Who did Italy beat 3-1 in the final of the 1982 World Cup?

142. Who scored the third Italian goal in the 1982 World Cup Final?

143. What was the name of the World Cup winning captain in 1982?

144. Who beat France 3-2 to finish third in 1982?

145. Which stadium hosted the 1982 World Cup Final?

146. Which African team, known as 'The Indomitable Lions, made its World Cup debut in 1982?

147. Which team from the Middle East made its one and only appearance at the 1982 World Cup?

148. Which English player scored the fastest goal of the 1982 World Cup?

149. Which country became the first to progress to Round 2 in a World Cup without winning a game?

150. Which French player was carried off unconscious in the 1982 World Cup Semi Final?

151. Which country did former European Footballer of the Year Kevin Keegan make his one and only World Cup appearance against as a substitute in Round 2?

152. Who was the Brazilian captain during the 1982 World Cup?

153. Which team finished top of group 5 in Round 1 of the 1982 World Cup? *A: Honduras B: Spain C: Northern Ireland D: Yugoslavia*

154. Who beat reigning European champions West Germany 2-1 in a first round match in 1982?

155. Which cartoon character was adopted by FIFA as its Fair Play Mascot before the 1982 World Cup?

# Mexico - 1986

156. Which country was originally chosen to host the 1986 World Cup but had to withdraw 4 years prior to the competition?

157. Who did Argentina beat 3-2 in the final of the 1986 World Cup?

158. Who scored the deciding goal in the 1986 World Cup Final?

159. What was the name of the World Cup winning captain in 1986?

160. Who did France beat 4-3 after extra time to finish third in the 1986 World Cup?

161. Which stadium hosted the 1986 World Cup Final?

162. Who won the Golden Boot in 1986?

163. How many hat-tricks were scored during the 1986 World Cup?

164. How many players did Argentina have in the All Star team of 1986?

165. Who managed the Scotland team at the 1986 World Cup following the untimely death of Jock Stein?

166. Which club was Karl Heinz Rummenigge playing for at the time of the 1986 World Cup?

167. Which English player was sent off in a first round match against Morocco?

168. Who scored the winning goal for West Germany in their 1-0 victory over Morocco in Round 2?

169. How many goals did Canada score on their first and so far only appearance at a World Cup in 1986?

170. Which European country made its first appearance at a World Cup in 1986?

# Italy - 1990

171. Who did West Germany beat 1-0 in the final of the 1990 World Cup?

172. Who scored the only goal in the 1990 World Cup Final?

173. Who became the only man to manage and captain a World Cup winning team in 1990?

174. Who did Italy beat 2-1 in the 3$^{rd}$ / 4$^{th}$ Place Play Off?

175. Which city hosted the opening game of the 1990 World Cup?

176. Who won the Golden Boot and Golden Ball in 1990?

177. Which country was banned from competing at the 1990 World Cup for fielding over age players in the FIFA World Youth Championship the previous year?

178. How many penalty shoot-outs were there during the 1990 World Cup?

179. Which West German player was sent off in their 2-1 victory over Holland in the 'Round of 16'?

180. Which country won the FIFA Fair Play Award in 1990?

181. Which team became the first from Africa to reach the quarter finals?

182. Who became the first African player to be named in the All Star Team in 1990?

183. Who was the Dutch captain at the 1990 World Cup?

184. How many red cards were there during the 1990 World Cup, setting a new record up to that point?

185. Who was the oldest player at the 1990 World Cup?

# USA - 1994

186. Who scored the only goal for Germany in their 1-0 win over Bolivia in the opening game of the 1994 World Cup?

187. Who did Brazil beat on penalties in the final of the 1994 World Cup?

188. What was the name of the World Cup winning captain in 1994?

189. Who did Sweden beat 4-0 in the 3$^{rd}$ / 4$^{th}$ Place Play Off?

190. Which stadium hosted the 1994 World Cup Final?

191. Who won the Golden Ball for 'Player of the Tournament' in 1994?

192. Which team became the first winners of 'The most entertaining team' award, as voted for by the public?

193. Which African team, known as the 'Super Eagles' qualified for their first World Cup in 1994?

194. Which goalkeeper was the first recipient of the 'Yashin Award' in the 1994 World Cup?

195. What was the name of the Colombia captain in the 1994 World Cup?

196. Which team finished top of group E in 1994? *A: Italy B: Ireland C: Norway D: Mexico*

197. Who was the coach of Switzerland for the 1994 World Cup?

198. Who beat Argentina 3-2 in the 'Round of 16' in 1994?

199. Which country scored the most goals during the 1994 World Cup?

200. Who scored a hat-trick for Argentina in their 4-0 demolition of Greece in Round 1 in 1994?

# France - 1998

201. Who did France beat 3-0 in the final of the 1998 World Cup?

202. Who scored the third goal for France in the 1998 World Cup Final?

203. What was the name of the World Cup winning captain in 1998?

204. Which country finished third in its first appearance at a World Cup in 1998?

205. Which stadium hosted the 1998 World Cup Final?

206. Who was the top goal scorer in 1998?

207. Which brothers both made it on to the All Star team of the 1998 World Cup?

208. Who won the 'Yashin award' for best goalkeeper in the 1998 World Cup?

209. Who scored the first ever 'golden goal' in a World Cup match in the 2$^{nd}$ round of 1998?

210. How many non-European teams made it through to the Quarter Finals in 1998?

211. Which team finished top of group D in 1998? *A: Bulgaria B: Nigeria C: Paraguay D: Spain*

212. Who was the coach of England at the 1998 World Cup?

213. Which team did Zinedine Zidane get sent off against in the first round of 1998?

214. Which Caribbean team, known as the 'Reggae Boyz', made its debut at the World Cup in 1998?

215. Who scored an 89th minute winner for Holland against Argentina in their epic 1998 World Cup Quarter Final?

# Japan and South Korea - 2002

216. Who beat the reigning champions France in the opening game of the 2002 World Cup?

217. Who did Brazil beat 2-0 in the final of the 2002 World Cup?

218. Who scored both goals for Brazil in the 2002 World Cup Final?

219. What was the name of the World Cup winning captain in 2002?

220. Who did Turkey beat 3-2 in the 3$^{rd}$ / 4$^{th}$ Place Play Off?

221. Which city hosted the 2002 World Cup Final?

222. Which country won the FIFA award for 'Most Entertaining Team' in 2002?

223. Which country won the FIFA Fair Play award in 2002?

224. Which Asian team made its first World Cup appearance in 2002?

225. Who became the first goalkeeper to win the Golden Ball in 2002?

226. Which country scored the most goals during the 2002 World Cup?

227. Which team finished top of group G in 2002? *A: Croatia B: Ecuador C: Italy D: Mexico*

228. Which European coach was in charge of South Korea during the 2002 Finals?

229. How many European teams made it through to the quarter finals in 2002?

230. Who did Germany beat 8-0 in the first round of the 2002 World Cup?

# Germany - 2006

231. Who did Italy beat on penalties in the final of the 2006 World Cup?

232. Who was the only player to miss a penalty in the shootout?

233. What was the name of the World Cup winning captain in 2006?

234. Who did Germany beat 3-1 in the 3$^{rd}$ / 4$^{th}$ Place Play Off?

235. Which stadium hosted the 2006 World Cup Final?

236. Which player finished the tournament as the highest goal scorer in 2006?

237. Which African team reached the quarter final in 2006?

238. Who was the first official recipient of the Young Player of the Tournament award in 2006?

239. Who was the coach of Holland during the 2006 World Cup?

240. Which country scored the most goals during the 2006 World Cup?

241. Who won the Golden Ball in 2006?

242. Who scored the winning goal for Italy 5 minutes into injury time in their 1-0 victory over Australia in the 'Round of 16'?

243. Which country, formerly part of the Soviet Union, made its independent debut in 2006?

244. Who was the final recipient of the 'Yashin award' for best goalkeeper of the tournament in 2006?

245. Dutch coach Leo Beenhaker was in charge of which World Cup debutant in 2006?

# South Africa - 2010

246. Who did Spain beat 1-0 after extra time in the final of the 2010 World Cup?

247. Who scored the only goal for Spain in the 2010 World Cup Final?

248. What was the name of the World Cup winning captain in 2010?

249. Who did Germany beat 3-2 in the 3rd / 4th Place Play Off?

250. Which city hosted the 2010 World Cup Final?

251. Who won the Golden Ball for Player of the Tournament in 2010?

252. Which goalkeeper won the 'Golden Gloves' award at the 2010 World Cup?

253. Who scored the winning goal for Spain in their 1-0 win over Portugal in the 'Round of 16'?

254. Which team won the FIFA Fair Play trophy in 2010?

255. Who was the manager named in the 'All Star Team' of 2010?

256. Which South American country reached the quarter finals for the first time in their history?

257. How many Spanish players were named in the 'All Star Team' of 2010?

258. Who was the only player to score a hat-trick at the 2010 World Cup?

259. Which German player was voted Best Young Player of the 2010 World Cup?

260. What was the score at the time when Frank Lampard's 'goal' was controversially not awarded against Germany?

# Goal Scorers

261. Who is the all time leading goal scorer in World Cup Finals up to 2010?

262. Which player once served a two year suspension from football prior to winning a Golden Boot?

263. Who holds the record for most goals scored in a single World Cup?

264. Who was the only player to score in every round of the World Cup, including the final?

265. Who is the youngest goal scorer in a World Cup Final?

266. Name the only player to score a hat-trick in a World Cup Final?

267. Which Russian scored 5 goals in one match at the 1994 World Cup?

268. Which European team was Mario Kempes playing for at the time of the 1978 World Cup?

269. Who is the oldest player to score a goal at a World Cup Finals?

270. How many times has a Brazilian player won the Golden Boot?

271. In which year did Marques Ademir win the Golden Boot?

272. Which country has scored the most goals in World Cup history up to 2010?

273. Besides Pele, who is the only other player to have scored in four different World Cup tournaments?

274. Who was the first player to score a penalty in a World Cup Final?

275. Which striker, known as 'The Vulture', became the first man since Eusebio in 1966 to score four goals in one match at the 1986 World Cup?

# World Cup Stadiums and Venues

276. Which city hosted the first ever World Cup match in 1930?

277. What name is the 'Stadio Giuseppe Meazza' more commonly known as?

278. Which city hosted the opening World Cup game of 2002?

279. In which US state would you find the 'Pontiac Silverdome' the first indoor stadium used in a World Cup?

280. What is the only stadium up to 2010 to have hosted the World Cup final twice?

281. Which World Cup Final stadium was often referred to as 'The Twin Towers'?

282. Which stadium holds the record attendance for a World Cup match?

283. How many stadiums were used during the inaugural World Cup of 1930?

284. In which city would you find the 'Nelson Mandela Bay' stadium?

285. Which World Cup host city has had the largest population?

286. Which NFL team would you find playing at Soldier Field, venue of the 'Round of 16' match between Germany and Belgium in 1994?

287. Which European club team play at the World Cup venue, the Allianz Arena stadium?

288. In which year did the 'Stadium of the National Fascist Party' host the World Cup Final?

289. How many stadiums were used for the 2010 World Cup?

290. Which World Cup had the lowest ever cumulative attendance of 358,000?

# World Cup Firsts

291. Which country was the first and only one to have to qualify as hosts?

292. Which country scored the first ever goal in a World Cup in 1930?

293. Which team did Manuel Rosas play for, the first player to score a penalty at the World Cup in 1930?

294. Who was the first person to win the World Cup as a player and a coach?

295. What year did the first ever penalty shoot-out take place?

296. Which team beat Mexico 3-1 in 1978 to become the first African nation to win a match at the World Cup?

297. Who beat Italy 1-0 in 1966 to record the first victory for an Asian nation at the World Cup?

298. Which nation did Bert Patenaude play for, the first player to score a hat-trick at the World Cup in 1930?

299. In which year was the first World Cup Final when at least one of Argentina, Brazil, Germany or Italy didn't feature?

300. In which year did Gianluca Pagliuca of Italy become the first goalkeeper to be sent off in a World Cup?

301. Which country did Ernst Lörtscher play for, the first player to score an own goal at the World Cup in 1938?

302. Jean Langenus refereed the first World Cup final in 1930, but from which European country did he come from?

303. Which country did Mario de Las Casas play for, the first player to be sent off in the World Cup in 1930?

304. What was the year the World Cup Final first went into extra time?

305. Which country did Juan Basaguren play for, the first player to score a goal as a substitute at the World Cup in 1970?

# World Cup Milestones

306. Which player has made most appearances at a World Cup with 25?

307. Who beat Switzerland 7-5 in 1954 in the World Cup's highest scoring match?

308. Which country scored the 500$^{th}$ goal in World Cup history in 1958?

309. Who was the only team to score 10 goals in a single match in 1982?

310. Which World Cup holds the record for the total cumulative attendance of 3,587,538?

311. Which country has appeared in the most semi-finals at the World Cup?

312. Which team scored 27 goals, the most in a single World Cup in 1954?

313. Who scored for Turkey after 11 seconds in 2002 to record the fastest goal ever scored at a World Cup?

314. Marcus Allback scored the 2000$^{th}$ World Cup goal against England in 2006, which country was he playing for?

315. Which player has spent the most time on the field in the World Cup at 2,217 minutes?

316. Which player has won the most matches at a World Cup, 16 in total?

317. Who became the youngest ever player in World Cup history in 1982?

318. Which country has lost the most matches at the World Cup?

319. Which World Cup legend has made most appearances as captain at a World Cup with 16?

320. Which Italian goalkeeper went 517 minutes without conceding a goal, a World Cup record?

# World Cup Legends

321. Artur Antunes Coimbra is better known as which Brazilian legend?

322. How old was Bobby Moore when he was first made England captain?

323. Which other country did Hungary's Ferenc Puskas represent 4 times late in his career?

324. Which former South American Footballer of the Year scored 10 World Cup goals for Peru in two different World Cup's in the 1970's?

325. Which club was Zinedine Zidane playing for at the time of the 1998 World Cup?

326. How many World Cups did Johan Cruyff play in?

327. Which Italian player became the oldest winner of the World Cup in 1982?

328. How many World Cup games did Franz Beckenbauer play in during his career?

329. Which country did Diego Maradona get sent off against in the 1982 World Cup?

330. Who is the only captain to lose two World Cup Finals?

331. Which Brazilian club side was Pele playing for throughout his World Cup career?

332. Which French club did Michel Platini play for before joining Juventus?

333. How many goals did Eusebio score in his one and only World Cup in 1966?

334. Which Italian defender won the World Cup as an 18 year old in 1982 and played his final World Cup game in 1998, having captained his side in 1990?

335. Which Brazilian was known as 'The Little Bird'?

# World Cup Trivia

336. How many different nations have won the World Cup up to 2010?

337. What is the name of the Greek 'Goddess of Victory' who is depicted in the original Jules Rimet Trophy?

338. Which cricket legend also played in the football World Cup qualifiers in the 1970's?

339. Out of the 19 World Cup's so far, how many have been won by the host nation?

340. Which country have qualified for the World Cup 8 times but never progressed beyond the first round?

341. Which year was the only World Cup where Brazil did not win at least one match?

342. Which country has been runner up the most times without actually becoming champions?

343. In which year was the first World Cup mascot introduced?

344. Which famous Tennis player's uncle played in three World Cups for his country?

345. Can you name the first English player to score in 3 consecutive World Cups?

346. How many days did the World Cup trophy go missing in England before being found by a dog named Pickles?

347. In which year did the World Cup first have 32 teams?

348. Lucien Laurent is the first player in World Cup history to do what?

349. In which year did the first brothers win the World Cup?

350. What did the United Arab Emirates players receive for each goal they scored at the 1990 World Cup?

# Answers

# Uruguay - 1930

1. Argentina
2. 13
3. Montevideo
4. Argentinian
5. 18
6. Argentina
7. 7
8. Jules Rimet
9. C: USA
10. Yugoslavia

# Italy - 1934

11. Czechoslovakia

12. 16

13. Rome

14. Germany

15. Czechoslovakian

16. Italy

17. 0

18. Egypt

19. 0

20. B: USA

# France - 1938

21. Hungary

22. 15

23. Brazil

24. 9, Antibes, Bordeaux, Le Havre, Lille, Marseille, Paris, Reims, Strasbourg, Toulouse

25. Brazilian

26. Hungary

27. Dutch East Indies (Indonesia)

28. Cuba

29. Spain

30. B: Poland

# Brazil - 1950

31. Maracana

32. 13

33. Brazil

34. Sweden

35. 6, Rio De Janeiro, Recife, Sao Paulo, Belo Horizonte, Curitiba, Porto Alegre

36. Brazilian

37. Japan

38. D: Brazil

39. India

40. England

# Switzerland - 1954

41. Hungary
42. Austria
43. Berne
44. Hungarian
45. Spain
46. Hungary
47. Ferenc Puskas of Hungary
48. South Korea
49. Mexico
50. Uruguay

# Sweden - 1958

51. Sweden

52. Mario Zagallo

53. French, Maurice Guigue

54. France

55. 12

56. 6

57. Billy Wright

58. Czechoslovakia

59. 3

60. Italy

61. Brazil

62. D: West Germany

63. Wales

64. 17

65. Real Madrid

# Chile - 1962

66. Czechoslovakia

67. Amarildo

68. Yugoslavia

69. Garrincha of Brazil

70. Colombia

71. Bulgaria

72. 4

73. Brazil

74. 2, Giorgio Ferrini and Mario David of Italy

75. Czechoslovakia

76. 6

77. D: West Germany

78. Argentina

79. 4

80. 7

# England - 1966

81. Germany

82. Martin Peters

83. Bobby Moore

84. Portugal

85. Goodison Park

86. Bulgaria

87. Eusebio of Portugal

88. 4

89. North Korea

90. 89

91. Bobby Charlton

92. Swiss, Gottfried Dienst

93. 0, they formally withdrew in protest at a FIFA ruling requiring them to play off against an Asian team

94. Portugal

95. 4

# Mexico - 1970

96. Italy

97. Jairzinho

98. Carlos Alberto

99. Uruguay

100. Azteca, Mexico City

101. Gerd Muller of West Germany

102. Peru

103. 0

104. 2, both scored by Gerd Muller

105. Pele of Brazil

106. 5

107. 3

108. Mexico

109. Morocco

110. 4

# West Germany - 1974

111. Holland

112. Franz Beckenbauer

113. English, Jack Taylor

114. Poland

115. Munich at the Olympiastadion

116. Grzegorz Lato of Poland

117. Rinus Michels

118. The Socceroos

119. East Germany

120. Billy Bremner

121. Johan Cruyff of Holland

122. 9

123. Haiti

124. Zaire

125. Sepp Maier

# Argentina - 1978

126. Holland

127. Mario Kempes

128. Daniel Pasarella

129. Italy

130. Estadio Monumental in Buenos Airies

131. Mario Kempes

132. Mexico

133. Berti Vogts

134. 1, only the final and 3$^{rd}$ / 4$^{th}$ Place Play Off were 'knockout games'

135. Argentina

136. *D: Austria*

137. Peru

138. Barcelona

139. Argentina

140. Tunisia

# Spain - 1982

141. West Germany

142. Marco Tardelli

143. Dino Zoff

144. Poland

145. Santiagao Bernabeu in Madrid

146. Cameroon

147. Kuwait

148. Bryan Robson

149. Italy

150. Patrick Batiston

151. Spain

152. Socrates

153. C: Northern Ireland

154. Algeria

155. Sport Billy

# Mexico - 1986

156. Colombia

157. West Germany

158. Jorge Burruchaga

159. Diego Maradona

160. Belgium

161. Azteca Stadium in Mexico City

162. Gary Lineker

163. 4

164. 1, Diego Maradona

165. Alex Ferguson

166. Inter Milan

167. Ray Wilkins

168. Lothar Mattheus

169. 0

170. Denmark

# Italy - 1990

171. Argentina

172. Andreas Brehme

173. Franz Beckenbauer

174. England

175. Milan, the San Siro

176. Salvatore (Toto) Schillachi of Italy

177. Mexico

178. 4

179. Rudi Voller

180. England

181. Cameroon

182. Roger Milla

183. Ruud Gullit

184. 16

185. Peter Shilton of England

# USA - 1994

186. Jurgen Klinsmann

187. Italy

188. Dunga

189. Bulgaria

190. Pasadena Rose Bowl in Los Angeles

191. Romario of Brazil

192. Brazil

193. Nigeria

194. Michel Preud'homme of Belgium

195. Carlos Valderamma

196. D: Mexico

197. Roy Hodgson

198. Romania

199. Sweden with 15

200. Gabriel Batistuta

# France - 1998

201. Brazil

202. Emmanuelle Petit

203. Didier Deschamps

204. Croatia

205. Stade De France in Paris

206. Davor Suker of Croatia

207. Michael and Brian Laudrup of Denmark

208. Fabian Barthez of France

209. Laurent Blanc of France

210. 2, Brazil and Argentina

211. *B: Nigeria*

212. Glenn Hoddle

213. Saudi Arabia

214. Jamaica

215. Denis Bergkamp

# Japan and South Korea - 2002

216. Senegal

217. Germany

218. Ronaldo

219. Cafu

220. South Korea

221. Yokohama, the International Stadium

222. South Korea

223. Belgium

224. China

225. Oliver Kahn

226. Brazil with 18

227. D: Mexico

228. Guus Hiidink of Holland

229. 4

230. Saudi Arabia

# Germany - 2006

231. France

232. David Trezeguet

233. Fabio Cannavaro

234. Portugal

235. Olympiastadion, Berlin

236. Miroslav Klose of Germany

237. Ghana

238. Lukas Podolski of Germany

239. Marco Van Basten

240. Germany with 14

241. Zinedine Zidane of France

242. Francesco Totti of Italy

243. Ukraine

244. Gianluigi Buffon of Italy

245. Trinidad & Tobago

# South Africa - 2010

246. Holland

247. Andres Iniesta

248. Iker Casillas

249. Uruguay

250. Joahannesburg, Soccer City stadium

251. Diego Forlan of Uruguay

252. Iker Casillas of Spain

253. David Villa

254. Spain

255. Vicente Del Bosque of Spain

256. Paraguay

257. 6

258. Gonzalo Higuain of Argentina

259. Thomas Muller

260. 2-1

# Goal Scorers

261. Ronaldo

262. Paolo Rossi

263. Just Fontaine

264. Jairzinho

265. Pele

266. Geoff Hurst

267. Oleg Salenko

268. Valencia

269. Roger Milla

270. 4, 1938, 1950, 1962 and 2002

271. 1950

272. Brazil

273. Uwe Seeler of Germany

274. Andreas Brehme of Germany

275. Emilio Butragueno of Spain

# World Cup Stadiums and Venues

276. Montevideo in Uruguay

277. San Siro Stadium in Italy

278. Seoul

279. Michigan

280. The Azteca, Mexico City

281. Wembley

282. The Maracana, Rio De Janeiro

283. 3

284. Port Elizabeth, South Africa

285. Tokyo

286. Chicago Bears

287. Bayern Munich

288. 1934 (in Rome)

289. 10

290. Italy, 1934

# World Cup Firsts

291. Italy

292. France

293. Mexico

294. Mario Zagallo of Brazil

295. 1982

296. Tunisia

297. North Korea

298. USA

299. 2010

300. 1994

301. Switzerland

302. Belgium

303. Peru

304. 1934

305. Mexico

# World Cup Milestones

306. Lothar Mattheus of Germany

307. Austria

308. Scotland

309. Hungary

310. USA 1994

311. Germany (inc appearances as West Germany)

312. Hungary

313. Hakan Sukur

314. Sweden

315. Paolo Maldini of Italy

316. Cafu of Brazil

317. Norman Whiteside of Northern Ireland

318. Mexico

319. Diego Maradona of Argentina

320. Walter Zenga

# World Cup Legends

321. Zico

322. 22

323. Spain

324. Teofilio Cubillas

325. Juventus

326. 1

327. Dino Zoff

328. 18

329. Brazil

330. Karl-Heinz Rummenigge

331. Santos

332. St Etienne

333. 9

334. Giuseppe Bergomi

335. Garrincha

# World Cup Trivia

336. 8, Uruguay, Italy, Germany, Brazil, England, Argentina, France and Spain

337. Nike

338. Sir Vivian Richards

339. 6, 1930, 1934, 1966, 1974, 1978, 1998

340. Scotland

341. 1938

342. Netherlands

343. 1966

344. Rafa Nadal

345. David Beckham

346. 7 days

347. 1998

348. Score a goal in the World Cup, playing for France vs USA in 1930

349. 1954, the Walter's of West Germany

350. A Rolls Royce!

www.ingramcontent.com/pod-product-compliance
Lightning Source LLC
Chambersburg PA
CBHW031417040426
42444CB00005B/617